Flowers Long for Stars

제 이 詞伯淸宴,
2005. 6. 19
오 세 영

FLOWERS LONG FOR STARS

Poems by Oh Sae-Young

Translated by Clare You & Richard Silberg

TAMAL VISTA PUBLICATIONS

Tamal Vista Publications
19A Forest Street No. 31
Cambridge, MA
02140

www.tamalvista.com

ISBN: 0-917436-07-5
Library of Congress Control Number: 2004115970

Special thanks to
Lee Young-Jun & Lee Sukja
for helping prepare the manuscript.

Designed by Wayne de Fremery

Published with a generous grant from

THE DAESAN FOUNDATION

In Memory of
Ok-Koo Kang Grosjean

CONTENTS

INTRODUCTION

Oh Sae-Young is an honored poet in his homeland of
Korea. Born in 1942, he is, in his early sixties, the author of
eleven books of poems and seventeen books of criticism.
While that is certainly a respectable body of work for a
major literary figure, Professor Oh's work, both in prose and
in poetry, is marked, not by its sweep, but by its depth and
concision.

In this volume Clare You and I, Korean native-speaker
and scholar and American poet, have collaborated to
bring a generous sampling of Professor Oh's poetry to an
American audience. We've tried to translate the poems into
an immediate, relatively informal English, to open them
out to an American taste for the casual and easy, but at the
same time, in that complex bridging and balancing inherent
in all translation, we've worked to keep the poems in touch
with the formal simplicity and ceremony that characterize,
enspirit the original poems.

Let's take a look, then, at one of his most famous poems,

"Dish," which appeared in the collection *Beyond Love,*
published in 1990.

DISH

A broken dish
becomes blades.

At the heart of balance
the force that cuts across
breaks circle into point
opens the cold eye
of reason.

Ah, the shards that
lie waiting for blind love.
I am barefoot now,
flesh waiting to be cut.
A soul that grows deep in the wound.

A broken dish
becomes blades.
All that is broken
becomes blades.

The poem in our English version immediately
distinguishes itself from the modal American poem, what
I call the American 'mainline'. That mainline style, the

style that predominates in our literary magazines and anthologies, is written in a conversational tone, the written illusion of informal speech. The lyric 'I' of the poet is usually front and center, the time and place of the 'speaking' usually specified, grounded in the poem's sensuous details, and the poem is a conversational slice, the spotlighting of this almost casual selection, the poem, from an ongoing intimate speech begun before the poem's beginning and continuing after it ends.

Professor Oh's poem distinguishes itself from this American modality at almost every point. Its tone is formal, the feel of the language composed, definitely 'written'. The 'I' of the poem appears fleetingly, almost shyly, in this procession of formal, essentially impersonal, language. And the reader isn't localized in time and place. The site of this writing is ideal; were this a Western poem, we might say that the dish it takes as its symbol is the Platonic ideal of a dish. And there's nothing casual, 'slice of life' about the way the poem frames itself. "Dish" is lapidary, ceremonial, in its beginning and ending, its first two lines repeating themselves verbatim in the first two lines of the concluding quatrain whose last two lines move the poem's opening statement a step further into generality, so that the whole poem takes a figure that we might think of as a circle with a coda.

And the poem's subject matter orbits, if you'll permit me that figure, the question of form and the dangers that attend its 'breaking'. The poem treats us to the idea of form as the 'balancing' of the chaotic forces that inhabit nature, so that when form is broken, chaos is released again: "A broken dish/ becomes blades."

But "Dish" is also more complex and more mysterious than my sententious explication of it. And that complexity and mystery seem to me the crux of Oh Sae-Young's talent and importance as a poet, as if they, themselves, took part in form and yet took part, also, in the chaotic forces that form seeks to tame in the fragile existence of dishes, of formal gardens, of our own form-seeking, but also lurkingly chaotic and dangerous lives.

What, for instance, does the "cold eye/ of reason" mean here? Wouldn't it be more natural to think of the whole dish, and its circular form, as the sentinels of reason? Yet in Professor Oh's poem reason opens its cold eye, eye of an eagle, when the circle breaks. Does that mean that art takes its being from another force than reason? And isn't there something essentially 'right', that makes us shiver in assent, in reason's association here with the "point," or the cut of a 'blade,' rather than with the unifying circle?

And who is this 'I' that speaks here, interlude in the poem's 'Platonic' drama? Why does he 'wait to be cut'? That brief, 'I'-based speaking is immediately followed by the line, "A soul that grows deep in the wound." Are we to read that line as an apposition? It's separated from what the 'I' says by a period, though. Is the line in paratactical relation to what the 'I' says, then? In other words, is the "soul" here the soul of that speaker, or is it some other soul, unspecified, soul of the eagle opening its 'reasonable' eye perhaps? The poem never answers these questions. They live, wild, within its hieratic language and lend it the strength of their "blind love."

In 1984, Oh Sae-Young was awarded the Nokwŏn Award, one of the many honors and awards he's received in his career. The Nokwŏn Award is the highest Buddhist honor in poetry, yet it strikes me as part of the refractory, riddling nature of his work—that complexity and mystery that I'm saying I value most, as the de-forming gleam in his un-reasonable eye—that this celebrated, Buddhist-influenced poet writes so memorably, not about peace and the release from desire, but about the longings of love and even, as here in his poem "Knife," about the creative power of "hate":

Knife
(from *Burning Water*)

You can never bring it out
without carving it.
Wooden doll
standing before the sharp blade,
you take a knife in the neck,
but death is perfection to you.
In the flurry of the fallen shavings
a dazzling body appears.
Consciousness clarifies
in hate's burning eyes.
Captive in the darkness
take the knife's thrust.
This could be the knife that
lit up Chaos in the Beginning.

How strange that poem is, for me, and haunting. It
hovers, in my understanding of it, somewhere between an
inverted love poem, almost a voodoo spell, and the more
ideal plane of a creation myth. But creation, here, isn't
ascribed to divine love or a more impersonal ordering
principle, but to "hate's burning eyes." Just as in "Dish"
reason's cold eye opens when the dish breaks, "consciousness
clarifies" in this poem through the dark passion of the

knife's blade. Again, this poem is ambiguous, mysterious, "captive in the darkness."

I Saw You

I saw you.
From outside the gate,
from outside the closed universe.
I saw you
from the tip of a branch,
from the edge of the dark sky,
I saw you.
I saw the fog, the snowy evening light,
the footsteps filled with light.
Wind that wailed in the white-birch woods
now stirs the locks behind my ears.
A broken flute
buried in the snow.
I saw you
from outside the gate,
from outside the closed universe.

I saw you,
one star, one bird,
my despairing eyes watching you.

If there's peace in that poem, repose, it's the peace of despair. I wouldn't call it a peaceful poem at all, though, but a poem of numbed longing. The poet has become "A broken flute/ buried in the snow." But the reader senses that numbness won't last. The speaker, the 'I' of this poem, more a singer, imaged in the stilled instrument, has found no freedom, no release from this love. The captivity is expressed in the poem's refrain: "I saw you … I saw you … I saw you …" We know that the anguish of this lost love will come flooding back like the 'phantom pain' from an amputated limb.

So Professor Oh's poems seem to me most at home, most powerful and expressive, not in realms of enlightenment, in the clarity and repose of nonattachment, but in the human wrestlings, longings, passions, that take place halfway on the ladder of consciousness, half in darkness, half in light.

But there are many kinds of poems in this book, a spectrum of moods, images, stances. I've probably focused on the poems that most answer my own taste. Let's close this introduction with a look at a poem, then, more obviously meditational, the sort of poem that a secular American like me would be likely to think of as 'Buddhist'.

MINDLESSLY

At the foot of
    the mountain
    bright in fall colors, stands
    a cracked boulder
under which lies
    a crumbling Buddha stone.
Beneath that flows
    a clear, fresh
    spring.
A forget-me-not
    bows to the deep blue sky
    mindlessly.

Fall

frost.

Simple, lovely, peaceful. We move in and in beneath the
crackedness and stony crumble to the clear spring. The
setting is humble, a no place special, that gleams, still, with
the specialness that is every place we really look at. The
poem says Buddha's name. The flower bows to the sky
"mindlessly," as we would if we could attain the 'no mind'
the poem points to quietly.
    And yet—is it just my psychologism, my need for
complexity?—I feel an undercurrent of sad longing. For me

there's a subtle doubleness that eddies across the peace, a doubleness I ascribe to the richness, almost the orneriness, of Oh Sae-Young's writing. I follow the poem in and in to the flower bowing to the sky, "blue," "deep." Then those last two words, "Fall," a season I, at any rate, associate with sadness, "frost," moving toward winter, toward the dead of the year. I feel a sudden yearning; I feel more lost than found.

—Richard Silberg

FROM *The Darkest Evening* 1982

CONTRADICTORY DIRT

The plate made from dirt
will return to dirt,
it will surely be broken
one day.

At the moment
we feast to the glory of life,
it shatters
a broken plate.
Men die once.

Kneaded with water, burnished by fire
at last, dirt comes alive.
All men
soak in water and
burn in fire.

I would be a piece of a plate
if destruction
became perfect after the break.

The contradictory plate,
made from dirt
to return to dirt.

WITHERED HANDS

Even after I am deep asleep
the laundry

keeps guard in darkness.
Withered hand that clutches
the loose line of fate.

It gives up
its body heat
cast before pure emptiness.

Though the stillness of night
is a world for winds,
outside the window of the wakened universe

laundry
casts a line
into the darkness of space.

His absolute act,
he, who gives up his body.

EMPTY SPACE

I fill up
the fountain pen
with ink.

Filled and filled again,
space remains
for the line of verse
that turns into flowers when I call you, you,
that turns
into stars when I call you,
you.

Everyone
lives in that space,
I draw a triangle of love and hate
in empty space,

put two dots
in empty space.

Isn't there ink that fills the space
between thoughts and things?
Ink that erases
winds wailing through boughs,
emptiness whispering near the ear.

Filled and filled again
space remains in the pen,
everyone
lives in empty space.

DREAMING SICKNESS

The girl was sick.
In slanting sunshine
she dreamed Africa.
A lion was
running the hot sandy horizon,
the girl was dreaming of love.
Listening to the radio that
breathes at the world's edge
in sleepless night
she knew how to cry
like rain soothing the stricken world.
Reading a love story,
she saw life and art steeped
in wine-glass pessimism.
Blue waves
break on the African coast where
a lion dozes.
The girl was not afraid
of approaching death,
just wished to see
how her only hope
would work out in this world.
While people were lighting the lamp
in the dark streets,
the girl was dreaming.
She sank deeply
into her dream.

WINTER DIARY

The picture frame,
there is peace in the photo there.

Through the fresh strands of my wife's hair
sunbeams chatter
while the coltish child squirts water in play.

Beside the calligraphy, a limp flower, or is it
a doll tilting her head?
She tilts her head, eyeing the seashore where
a lone fisherman mends his net.

As I flip a page of my torn life,
January 4th, 1971,
cloudy.
I write and tear up letters
listening to the radio all day.

The coltish child plays with water
across frozen time; the sea breeze
swells the waves and scatters their white foam
over the sadness of my career.

A photo in the frame,
the peace within,
the face of my sleeping wife,
I saw summer
breaking over pale waves.

FROM *Unenlightened Love Songs* 1986

Knife

I hammered it
to make a dagger.
I hammered the soft iron
to forge a gleaming blade.

I heated the slack body,
A fever in my chest, ice on my forehead,
I quenched
my wretched life in water.

The world is
a furnace,
wrought iron that's
blind to love and
wakes in hatred,
a knife that
was forged by the hand of a foe,

I hammered it
to forge the blade,
to wake up the sleeping hatred.

THE FLUTE

On a lonely day
I played the flute.
Voice of the wind that
echoes in my empty heart.

Happiness, anger, sadness and joy,
the four holes broken.
Stroking the back
with withered hands,
lip meets lip.

The flute
makes melodies
only those who are thirsty.
Wings
soar because they are empty.

On a lonely day
I played the flute
sitting alone by the river.
My broken body is wet with rain,
the sounds of wind, waves,
the repeating sounds of wind that
echo empty space.

HIGH NOON

What frustrates you so, wisteria,
pouring out a mouthful of fragrance
at high noon on a summer's day
though no one is gossiping?
What do you mean
fluttering your leaves
through the windless air
though no one points a finger at you?
You holding a lamp
up to the sky at high noon.
A piece of cloud
floating above this realm of desire,

you who
lost your mind,
tired from calling and calling.

A MOUNTAIN BIRD

The woods are calling the woods and
the fields are calling the fields.
Calling trees to come naked,
calling withered wildflowers to come.
Across the river and over the knoll,
a lost way.
The world dreams by the steep rise and
a lone mountain bird is singing.
The way is far, the way is near.
Woods call themselves the way.
Fields call themselves the way.

THREE IN THE MORNING

Three in the morning
the river flows riverly,
the sea is sea blue,
pheasants nestle mate by mate.
Three in the morning,
it is the hour when
moonlit eyebrows drift,
the Milky Way wets hair behind ears, and
stars sparkle dreams in the forehead.
Awakened at three in the morning,
I recite the sutra.

One is many, many is one; following the teachings, I
understand the meaning; by the meaning I understand the
teachings; not-being is being, being is not-being; formlessness
is form and form has none; no-nature is nature and nature is
no-nature. ...

Ah, the words of the Garland Sutra, rush of the ebb tides
    surging in the heart,
    the rustle of oak leaves.

THE SOUND OF WIND

The sound of wind that
rides my body,
good-bye, farewell.
Moonlight fades over the ferry landing,
the voice of my love
fades across the river.

Rustle of oak leaves that
rides my body,
good-bye, farewell.
Starlight falling on the draw-string of your linen blouse,
sound of autumn rain that wets your eyelashes.

There are only rivers and winds in this world.
There are only the winds rippling your blouse draw-string.
There is only the river wetting your skirt.

Sound of waves
riding my body,
sound of autumn rain that
wets the dry riverbed.

Blue, Yellow, Green and Purple

Blue, yellow, green and purple,
each in its own color,
when I call their names, each blossoms,
the touch-me-nots, cockscombs, rose mosses, marvels-of-Peru.

Wanting to catch your beauty
on canvas, I spray colors.
Autumn is already
at the tip of my brush
one by one lamps light up in the windows.

The light lit by a touch-me-not.
The light lit by a rose moss. ...

Pole Star, Vega, Betelgeuse, Dog Star
world is a dizzy field of stars,
red jade, ruby, sapphire and emerald,
the gems that wake when called.

CREMATION

We buried it
like planting a flower seed.
With one eye in the heart,
reciting a sutra, memorizing an incantation
and kindling
the dry branches,
we buried a spark in the frozen soil.
Like dropping a flower seed,
that's how it was dropped,
a fall of tears on the soil.
If we look around, this world is an arid tidal flat
where a wooden ferry is rotting.
We let them fly,
a handful of ashes by the riverbank,
like scattering flower seeds.

I Saw You

I saw you.
From outside the gate,
from outside the closed universe.
I saw you
from the tip of a branch,
from the edge of the dark sky,
I saw you.
I saw the fog, the snowy evening light,
the footsteps filled with light.
Wind that wailed in the white-birch woods
now stirs the locks behind my ears.
A broken flute
buried in the snow.
I saw you
from outside the gate,
from outside the closed universe.

I saw you,
one star, one bird,
my despairing eyes watching you.

MIRROR

Trying to erase your image,
I look into the mirror
in a dim lamplight.
Trying to erase my image,
I watch the darkness,
rubbing my dull eyes.
Erasing an eyebrow, I kill my children,
erasing a lip, I kill my parents,
putting on makeup, I kill my master.
A mask with a mop of hair,
lets it fall.
The mop of hair and eyelashes
is weeping.
To kill children, to kill parents,
at last to kill myself,
putting on a mask
at midnight,
trying to erase your image,
I look into the mirror
under the dim lamplight.

FROM *Burning Water* 1988

Earthly Food

You fly
only to come back down.
Birds,
wake from the egg,
just as you flutter your silver wings.
Though you put your faith in the sky,
though you believe only the sky is freedom,
you will never know without soaring into the air
what great despair freedom is.
A few grains
scattered in the muddy fields,
the food you dream about
is found only on earth.
Birds,
illogical birds.

CLIFF

It is a wild celebration,
the mountain staggers drunk,
wrapped in a tender green shawl
that covers its fresh body.
Trees huddle with trees,
leaves with leaves,
they whisper in sweet tongues.
Caught kissing, the mountain blushes.
Everyone bursts into laughter.
Returning from a long breakup,
spring spins with the joy of chance meeting.
The chiming of a silver chalice,
Clink!
Ice breaks in remote valleys.
Not knowing what to do on this bright spring day,
the cliff once again
cracks.

KNIFE

You can never bring it out
without carving it.
Wooden doll
standing before the sharp blade,
you take a knife in the neck,
but death is perfection to you.
In the flurry of the fallen shavings
a dazzling body appears.
Consciousness clarifies
in hate's burning eyes.
Captive in the darkness
take the knife's thrust.
This could be the knife that
lit up Chaos in the Beginning.

Rolling Stone

The caught stone
stuck in the ground
trembling in hatred
lies in wait like a trap,
a stumblingstone, but

the rolling stone
never
trips us.
Leaving its fate to the flowing currents,
when it finds itself in a flower bed, it plays with flowers,
when it finds itself in a puddle, it plays with the crabs.

The rolling stone
doesn't insist on its strength,
knows how to be broken.
It rolls along the road,
scuffing along by itself,
————whoops, a cliff!
Falling stone,
the road
to eternity,
the stone becomes sand at last,
sand that wallows along
in the dazzling sunshine.

The stuck stone becomes mud but
the rolling stone
becomes glittering sand by the seashore.

On a Blue Spring Day

If I went to the riverbank
would they still be shattered,
silvery days of my lost youth?
On a spring evening
flower petals fall gently in the breeze
and tears fall
on cold parting hands.
If I went to the seashore
could I find it?
Salt crystal that
sparkled in the dry sea-sand,
the diamond that was slipped
onto my trembling finger.

On a blue spring day
let's go to the riverbank.
On a yearning spring day
let's go to the seashore.

If You Are Tired of Longing

If you are tired of longing,
let us drink a cup of tea
sitting under the shadow of a blue wisteria.
Boiling passion sleeps now,
the flame is still.
Not a trace of cloud in the sky
held in a celadon teacup.
Who said love is a fever?
A sip of water that wets the parched lips
as dew gathers
on restless flower petals.

If you are tired of waiting,
let's share a cup of tea
under the blue shadow of wisteria.

A Summer Day

At midday in summer
even the winds are tinted blue,
leaves, like paintings,
cling to branches, and
the song of the cicada ceased long ago.
......

Glassy sunlight from the sky
is heavy,
high noon,
the whole world
sparkles in blue gems.

Unable to bear the smothering silence,
a smile,
the lotus blossom unfolds and
a frog on the clear pond
rolls its eyes
eavesdropping
on the sound.

BLACKOUT

There are sentences to be written
still.
The light blinks out.
I stare at the silence of
the cool filament
I can't write any more.
The last word
perhaps
could've been "good-bye"
but it has
no meaning.
The white heat charged with passion
is gone,
my body rolls in copper coil, and
electric wire droops outside the window.
I gaze
at distant starlight.
Still
a letter remains unwritten,
the word "good-bye" hangs.
The bulb blinks out
at the peak of the current,
leaving a word
to be written under starlight.
The pencil
snaps at midnight.

FROM *Beyond Love* 1990

DISH

A broken dish
becomes blades.

At the heart of balance
the force that cuts across
breaks circle into point
opens the cold eye
of reason.

Ah, the shards that
lie waiting for blind love.
I am barefoot now,
flesh waiting to be cut.
A soul that grows deep in the wound.

A broken dish
becomes blades.
All that is broken
becomes blades.

WITHERED FLOWERS

The flowers are withered,
the water has dried up,
only a broken vase
stands guard in the dark.

Ah, thirsty.
The broken body
wakes at three
fumbling for water on the night-table.
The vase is deaf.

The world is full of flowers
        each blooming for itself.
The crapemyrtle laughs ha, ha, ha.
The plantain lily laughs heh, heh, heh.

Awake at three,
a cracked vase
listens.

SPRING RIVER WATER

We've come as far as we can.
Now it's time to step down.
Leaving the
empty wagon,
we must go on.

Exhausting journey,
across the plains,
over the mountains,
we can see the other shore.
The wagon is useless
from here.

A log raft disappearing across the river,
yeo-i, yeo-i
this sick body out of breath,
yeo-i, yeo-i
the spring river slaps flatly.

Life is an empty wagon
standing on the river bank,
calling out to the vanishing raft,
yeo-i, yeo-i
as the spring river slaps flatly.

ONE IN THE MORNING

One in the morning,
the last train has pulled out.
A lone trash can keeps watch
on the plaza.

Whose tears did it dry once
that waiting—
the white handkerchief thrown away?

Whose pain did it soothe once
that letter
of crumpled passion?

Dreaming starlit world,
lonely trash can.

A sagging powerline,
that smoldering cigarette butt
tossed by the empty bench.

BEAST

Don't touch.
I'm a collapsing iron fence.
The sky I caged is now
an angry beast,
wildness
is loose now.

Sometimes,
clouds scudding across the sky
burst into rain storm.
Sweet wind
drums out its anger.
The dam on the lake
is cracked by
flood.

There Is Darkness in God's Sky, Too

Just as I scatter letters
    on blank paper
    a, b, c, d, …
God scatters stars
    in the night sky.
Why do we fear empty space?
The absolute nothingness, that space of God, he
    tries to fill with beams of light, …
But I
    try to fill it with words.
When I sprinkle letters
    a, b, c, d, … on blank paper,
these seeds that fall to the ground
become flowers, grasses
and trees, but
they, too, will return to empty space some day.
In the far distance between you and me
words
burn like the flames of a meteor.
Because there is light
in God's sky
there is darkness, too.

FROM *Flowers Long for Stars* 1992

A Letter

When a plant
buds
it's waiting for someone.

A hydrangea standing alone
in a dark alley on a bright spring day
withers little by little.

Petals drifting on the wind
like pieces of a torn letter,
flowers' shed petals are
last love letters sent
by plants tired of waiting.

If I used this flower petal for a stamp,
would they deliver the letter?
Sitting in the flower shade of late spring
I write my last letter
to you today.

Words of Farewell

Even if they are
last words,
how much more beautiful to say,
"Wait for me," than
"Let us part."
The parting, not in words
but in our eyes.
"Good-bye,"
as the hand is extended,
a flower petal casts its shade across your eyes.
My love that once whirled up in passion
now silently falling like petals.
We part in spring,
our autumn sorrow is yet to come.
Please, tell me to wait for you,
even
if they are your last words.

FAR SIGHTED

Distant things
are beautiful.
Rainbows, stars and the flowers on a cliff,
distant things
are beautiful
because my hand can't reach them.
My love,
don't be sad at parting.
At my age, this parting is
not parting, only
growing distant.
Now
I need glasses
to read your last letter.
Getting old is letting my loved ones
be far away.
It is knowing
how to watch you from a distance.

CHERRY BLOSSOMS

Death is forever,
you can't die twice.
What does not change
on this earth?
Like the woman
toasting eternity
kissing the suicide cup,
cherry blossoms
are shed all at once
at the height of their beauty.

The ceremony of death that denies the end,
art
of self-destructive passion.

MORNING GLORY

Flowers bloom
    in the asphalt
as well as the soil.

Shoulder to shoulder
    united arm in arm
Wa, Wa! They storm
    the barricade in pursuit of the sun.

No oppression stands
    against you.
Endless struggling vines
    climbing toward the blue sky,
you'd rather
    cover the walls with flowers.
Freedom!
Like the flags in the square after gun smoke has faded
    the wall is alive with climbers reaching for the light.

Our land's beautiful June Morning Glories,
all of them, rising.

— At the uprising of June 1986, Seoul

FEBRUARY

No month
goes as nicely
with the word, "already."
New Year's day seems only yesterday but
already it's February.
Don't let it pass
without looking over the plum blossom in the garden.
They
smile before you know it
from what used to be a vacant lot.
The world
shows up
only when it's called.
I stop on my walk
for suddenly
it's February as I take my fur coat off.
The month that says
things aren't what they seem to be.
No month
goes as nicely as February
with the word, "already."

MARCH

If I listen to
the running creek,
March
seems to go with slapping sounds
of women washing winter clothes.

If I listen to
the jostling of azalea bushes,
March
seems to go with shouts
of children running through the field.

If I listen to
the good earth sprouting seeds,
March
seems to go with suckling sounds
of babies.

Ah, facing the splendor of the sun
the green leaves wave their hands.
March
seems to go with freedom cries.
That day, they were shouting
at Aunae market place.

* The poem celebrates the March First independence movement of 1919.

November

Now is the season when the sun hangs low.
I look around,
everything is gone.
Where there should be flowers,
where there should be leaves,
only reeds stand in the empty field.
Season of frost,
before this icy blade
flowers with flowers, leaves with leaves
cast their lives
onto the naked ground.
Only the reeds lament their time
standing up to empty sky.
Winter's patience
wants to crumble dry
rather than rot.
Reeds
even when they stoop to earth
they stand up to the sky.
They buttress the sun.

FROM *Foolish Hegel* 1994

Airplane Ticket

Follow the road
to Rome or
to Paris as you travel, they say, but
when a man sets foot on the road
it's not always
to arrive at a place on the map.
On a spring afternoon
like flowers fading on a breath of wind
wafting into the skyway,
on an autumn evening
like leaves falling at odd moments
afloat in the Milky Way,
a man takes to the road because
tides swell
in his heart.
Life is only a dot on the map.
A map in hand
where shall I go?
Petal falling through the air,
to Rome or to Paris.
I buy an airplane ticket
on a spring afternoon.

TEARS

Water can burn, too, like fire.
Only those who have seen sorrow
know.
Look
at the blazing sunset
from the darkening seashore
on a summer day.
What grieves you so,
weeping 'til your eyes are red?

White crystals
settle on the salt flat
like dried tears streaking the cheeks.
Salt is the dead ember of sorrow.
If love is the light of fire blazing
sorrow is the burning light of water.
Tears silently kindling in your eyes
light
the darkness.

DRAMA

Standing water becomes a picture but
flowing water
becomes a language.

Lake with mountains,
sea with skies, water colors.
Eyes that gaze
up at desolate space.

That's why flowing water
tries to embrace
mountain and sky in words.
Its voices are large and small,
deep and shallow.

Water
streaming by thickets, whispers,
meeting the rapids, grumbles,
clashing with rocks, shouts.
Ah! It's a waterfall.

The fate of an actor who was
destroyed at the moment of passion,
that fall.
Drama is falling water.

Flowing water becomes prose but
water falling from a cliff
becomes drama.

COFFEE

Should I write I love you?
Should I write I hate you?
The pen trembles
before the silent notebook page.
I drink a cup of coffee
with an unsteady hand.
It's not sweet.
It's not bitter.
The flavor
blends them.
It's the right flavor
if sugar is added just so.
I don't like black coffee.
Like sugar melting in a cup
my senses dissolve in a cup of reason.
Drinking coffee at night alone
before the blank notebook page
I see myself.

LABOR

Summer day.
The farmer's coppery back
steaming with sweat
at the plow. Look.
The delicate beads of the sweat of labor
are lovelier
than dew on flower petals.
If night dews are the crystals of pleasure
drops of sweat are the crystals of labor.
In an instant
dews evaporate into the air, but
sweat becomes salt crystals.
Salt is a gem
made from our pain.
Let us sweat.
Gems last longer than dew.

FRUIT

Why must all fruits of the earth
be round?
Even the sweet berries of thorny bushes are
round.
Though the roots boring deep into the earth
are keen, and
the branches shooting high into the sky
are pointed,
the fruits that ripen and drop by themselves
have no edges.

A winsome apple,
crunch,
        we take a bite.
The biting teeth are sharp but
the bitten apple is soft.

Are you beginning to see that all
that lives and grows is round, and that
edible fruits have no edges?

Falling Leaves

Neither an exclamation nor a question mark,
there is now
only the period
to be placed.

One line of the poem written
with utter truth
waiting for its final period,
the tree stands
high on a crag.

How beautiful
are empty hands humbly waiting
with their best.
God needs to fill this space
with light and fragrance now.

The tree stands
up to the sky at last,
shedding the leaves and flowers
that it suffered to bloom.

Leaving a blank space,
I place a period
at the end of that long sentence.

EAVESDROPS

Winter's snow
      drips from the eaves.
Has spring come to the temple
      tucked deep in the valley?

Slap dash,
melting ice flows through the glens,
      runs, runs to the sea.

But no. Water
rises to the sky.
The rule
in water's realm
is that the lowest becomes the highest.

If I put my ear to the door and listen,
      I hear petals from bygone years
            scattering in air.
      I hear dew from last summer
            drip to the soil.

Things that fall
      really fly high,
only fire and ice remain on earth.

Let us open our hearts.
Let us be water and flow.
Let us head for the sea
on a fresh, green spring day.

MOUNTAIN PATH

Who made
    the path to the mountain?
The squirrels, the jack rabbits or
    our ancient grandma-bear?

In the grassy dark soil
the Bear Maiden's soft soles might have lightly
stepped
a blossom of edelweiss that
breathes forth its fragrance.
Who made the mountain path?
Why?
Maybe the wind,
wind from the mountains sweeping down to the sea.
Maybe the white clouds,
white clouds born in the mountains puffing the sky.
Where fields end, the mountain stands.
Where mountain ends, the sky goes on.
Following squirrels, following jack rabbits,
footsteps lead to the mountain,
onward, upward to the sky,
walking footsteps.

* Bear Maiden: the mythical mother of Koreans.

Spring Path

Here, a rice paddy,
there, a farm field.
Men draw lines to pave the road but
spring erases the lines on its way.
In the barley fields
fresh green sprouts,
in the mustard fields, too,
yellow florets burst out.
Zigzagging the banks of rice paddies and fields,
spring makes its way north.

Walking spring's path,
suddenly,
    my heart darts
    to erase
the Cease-fire Line.

FROM *Sky Mirrored in Tears* 1994

FAR AWAY

The lamplight across the river
     more than a flower blooming on the bluff;
the rainbow above the sea
     more than the lamplight across the river;
the stars in the sky
     more than the rainbow above the sea
     are lovely.

I'd rather be
     a poet who sits by the window looking at stars than
     a fawn crying at the edge of a cliff.

My love
     if I can't see you again
     why don't you go far away?

Being near yet so far
     is more distant than
     being far away yet so close.

My love
your nearness
     is sheer distance.

A Vacant Chair

The window,
    no butterflies, no hummingbirds
    glance in.
One tendril of ivy
    desperately
    climbs the red brick wall,
    tips its head and
    peeks in at the window.
A vacant chair,
    dusty,
    sitting in the empty room,
beneath it, buttercup, tulip and cyclamen burst into laughter.

Blinding light floods the audience,
standing ovation, whistling cheers.
Wakened by the fury of *Del Primo Pianto,*
the prima donna looks for him where
    he isn't.

One chair
empty in the full house.

ONE DAY

After the rain of angel-hair
fresh shoots of shepherd's purse turn green.
Through folds of damp grass
a flower-snake peers out with tiny eyes.

After the rain of angel-hair
sowthistle and wild thistle prick up,
the dry rapids of the stream
turn blue
today.

Oh, green swallow, what can I do?
A rusty hinge
flat on the gravel bed.
Ah, pretty green snake, what can I do?
A stone Maitraeya
lying in the mud.

What Am I?

What am I?
I do not know myself.
When I drew your face in my moist breath
on the window of a subway train
people called me
a fool.

When I groaned out your name
in the rainy plaza of the Seoul Train Station
people called me
a madman.

When I absent-mindedly wrote your name
on the streets of Chongno
people called me
a tramp.

Truly, what am I?
It is all right if you call me a puff of wind,
I will be your moist breath that
disperses in the air.

Flowers are flowers,
stars are stars but
what am I to you?

No Trace

Though rumors abound
there's no trace of you.
Some say you were in a tavern in Moogyo village,
some say you were on the theater streets of Chongno
and others say
they saw you at the L.A. airport.

Though rumors abound
you're nowhere.
Following a wagtail
where the wagtail goes
there's one lonely plantain flower.

Following a mountain sparrow
where the sparrow goes
there's one sad archilla-weed.

Following a nightjug
where the nightjug goes
there's a tender misty-blue
but
over my drooping shoulder as I turn away
the wagtail whispers,
have you seen the dew on plantain blossoms
basking in the May morning sun?

Behind my slumping back as I turn away
the mountain sparrow whispers,
have you seen the petals of archilla-weeds

evenly moist in the July shower?

At my dull ear as I turn away
a nightjug whispers,
have you seen the stalks of misty-blues
bleaching in September frost?

I Am Not Alone

You say I'm alone?
When the peony by the wall
was sprouting
pushing up through icy winter soil
I saw your warm hand there.

You say I'm alone?
When the green grapes in the backyard
ripened
each grape of the cluster beneath a clear sky
I saw your glance there.

You say I'm alone?
As the mums in the garden
burst into yellow blooms
I smelt your sweet breath there.

You say I'm alone?
How can I live in this world alone?
As the pine in the backyard
dropped a pine cone to the snow field
I heard your voice there.

On this day of clear sky
how can I live in this world alone
without you?

THE GATES OF HEAVEN

Crack!
Lightning
strikes from the parched sky.
The flash and clap are fierce.
Crack!
The shower
    stops
    as soon as the dark sky opens.
A rainbow hangs
    in the east.

The ladder of colors
you have lowered for me
    opens the gates of heaven.
How shall I climb it!
A tiny bug just woke up
    on the mottled rose petals
Flutte - r - r - r - s
    its wings at the sky.

FACE

Poems shouldn't
be written by a window but
facing a wall.
The sky is really a giant wall.
It is finer to be awakened by despair than
to be deceived by vain hope.
The lark's dream of soaring into the sky
and the pain of a fly cruising the wallpaper
are no different.
I'd rather be a ballpoint pen on a desk
writing in blood
digging into the wall.

Poems don't work
to open windows but
to tear down walls.
Today someone must be tearing down the wall,
lightning strikes in the arid sky.
At the moment of the flash
your face appears.

THE PAINTER

I will paint your lips
as a lotus blossom,
your nose as white jade,
your ears as crystal,
your eyebrows as a crescent moon.
But
I can't paint your eyes
because they shine too bright,
because your glance is too dazzling.
My love,
won't you please close your eyes for a moment
so I can look at you straight.
But   but
the love I painted is not my love,
because with closed eyes you are not you.
I cannot paint my love.

Outside the Gate

Where
are you hiding?
Trying to find you
I lingered
outside the gate of flowers
because you are beautiful.

—As I opened the gate of flowers, there was a scent; as I
opened the gate of scent, there was a wind; as I opened the
gate of wind, there was the sky; as I opened the gate of the
sky, there was the light; as I opened the gate of light, there
was the rainbow; as I opened the gate of the rainbow, it
rained; as I opened the gate of the rain, there was a tree; as I
opened the gate of the tree, again there were flowers.

Where are you hiding?
As always I stand
outside your gate.
All beauty stands inside.

MINDLESSLY

At the foot of
    the mountain
    bright in fall colors, stands
    a cracked boulder
under which lies
    a crumbling Buddha stone.
Beneath that flows
    a clear, fresh
    spring.
A forget-me-not
   bows to the deep blue sky
   mindlessly.

Fall

frost.

The Sound of Winter Rain

Alone, wakened by fever,
I nurse my thirst
in the empty ward of the dark night.
The ward is haunted
by the cold white light
of fluorescent bulbs shining on bed sheets,
the pale moth is fluttering on the white curtain.
If there is a ward for longing
it has to be white.
What time is it?
Waited for you 'til the end, but you did not return ...
The echo of slippers
in the hallway
coming close, so close, then fading away.

The sounds of winter rain falling on frozen soil.